T0014704

AMAZONIAN GIANT CENTIPEDE VS. BRAZILIAN WANDERING SPIDER

BY NATHAN SOMMER

TORQUE
TM

BELLWETHER MEDIA · MINNEAPOLIS, MN

Torque brims with excitement perfect for thrill-seekers of all kinds. Discover daring survival skills, explore uncharted worlds, and marvel at mighty engines and extreme sports. In *Torque* books, anything can happen. Are you ready?

This edition first published in 2024 by Bellwether Media, Inc.

Library of Congress Cataloging-in-Publication Data

LC record for Amazonian Giant Centipede vs. Brazilian Wandering Spider available at: https://lccn.loc.gov/2023042536

Editor: Suzane Nguyen   Designer: Josh Brink

Printed in the United States of America, North Mankato, MN.

TABLE OF CONTENTS

THE COMPETITORS

South America's **rain forests** are home to many **predators**. Some of them have deadly bites! Amazonian giant centipedes use theirs to **paralyze** their food.

The centipedes compete for food with Brazilian wandering spiders. These spiders use **venom** to defeat much larger enemies. Which deadly biter would win in a battle?

Amazonian giant centipedes are the world's largest centipedes. They grow up to 12 inches (30 centimeters) long! They have narrow bodies with up to 23 pairs of yellowish legs. Their heads have large **antennae**.

These centipedes live in northern South America. They are often found under wood or in soil. They also live in caves.

TAKING A BREATHER

Amazonian giant centipedes do not breathe through their mouths. They breathe through openings on the sides of their bodies!

AMAZONIAN GIANT CENTIPEDE PROFILE

0	3 INCHES	6 INCHES	9 INCHES	12 INCHES

LENGTH
UP TO 12 INCHES
(30 CENTIMETERS)

WEIGHT
UP TO 14.1 OUNCES
(400 GRAMS)

HABITAT

RAIN FORESTS

AMAZONIAN GIANT CENTIPEDE RANGE

■ RANGE

BRAZILIAN WANDERING SPIDER PROFILE

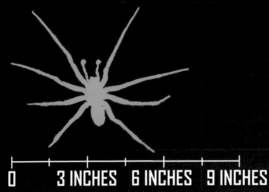

0   3 INCHES   6 INCHES   9 INCHES

LENGTH
UP TO 7 INCHES
(18 CENTIMETERS)

WEIGHT
UP TO 0.2 OUNCES
(6 GRAMS)

HABITAT

RAIN FORESTS

BRAZILIAN WANDERING SPIDER RANGE

■ RANGE

Brazilian wandering spiders are hairy. They can be as wide as 7 inches (18 centimeters) across. They have grayish-brown bodies and striped legs. Their jaws are red.

They wander the forest floor to hunt. This is how they got their name! They are found in parts of Central and South America.

BEHIND THE NICKNAME

Brazilian wandering spiders are also called banana spiders. They are often found hiding in bunches of bananas.

SECRET WEAPONS

Amazonian giant centipedes are fast. Their many legs help them chase **prey**. They use their spiny back legs to attack enemies who get too close!

CAVE HUNTERS

Amazonian giant centipedes hang upside down from cave ceilings. They do it to catch bats!

Brazilian wandering spiders are also speedy. They use their long legs to easily catch prey. The spiders raise their front legs to scare off enemies.

SIZE COMPARISON

AMAZONIAN GIANT CENTIPEDE
12 INCHES (30 CENTIMETERS)

BRAZILIAN WANDERING SPIDER
7 INCHES (18 CENTIMETERS)

0   3 INCHES   6 INCHES   9 INCHES   12 INCHES

MANDIBLES

The front two legs on Amazonian giant centipedes are called **mandibles**. These are sharp. The centipedes use these to catch and bite their prey.

Brazilian wandering spiders show their bright red jaws when threatened. This warns enemies to stay away. The spiders attack enemies who come too close.

SECRET WEAPONS

AMAZONIAN GIANT CENTIPEDE

MANY LEGS	MANDIBLES	VENOM

Amazonian giant centipedes pack a deadly bite. They deliver venom that quickly paralyzes prey. They use this to defeat small **mammals** like mice and bats.

SECRET WEAPONS

LONG LEGS

BRIGHT RED JAWS

VENOM

QUITE THE BITE

People bitten by Brazilian wandering spiders often feel ill. The bites can be deadly if people do not seek help!

Brazilian wandering spiders are one of the world's most venomous spiders. Their venom stops prey from moving. Bites from the spiders can even be deadly to humans!

ATTACK MOVES

Amazonian giant centipedes cannot see well. They use their antennae to locate nearby prey. They chase and **lunge** at prey once finding it.

Brazilian wandering spiders use **scare tactics** against predators. They raise their front legs high to show their red jaws. The color warns predators that they are venomous.

Amazonian giant centipedes bite prey once they catch it. Their venom instantly paralyzes most prey. They use their mandibles to bite and chew their meal.

Brazilian wandering spiders are **aggressive** hunters. The spiders hunt prey by both **ambush** and direct attacks. They chase prey. Then they **inject** it with venom.

READY, FIGHT!

An Amazonian giant centipede approaches a Brazilian wandering spider. The spider raises its legs. But this does not scare off the centipede!

The centipede lunges at the spider with its mandibles. But it misses! The spider bites the centipede. It escapes as the centipede is defeated by its venom. This deadly spider won today!

GLOSSARY

aggressive—ready to fight

ambush—to carry out a surprise attack

antennae—body parts on an animal's head that are used for sensing or smelling

inject—to force a fluid into something

lunge—to move forward quickly

mammals—warm-blooded animals that have backbones and feed their young milk

mandibles—jaw-like body parts that centipedes use to hold and bite food

paralyze—to make unable to move

predators—animals that hunt other animals for food

prey—animals that are hunted by other animals for food

rain forests—thick, green forests that receive a lot of rain

scare tactics—a fighting strategy in which one animal tries to make itself appear as large or scary as possible in hopes of scaring the other off

venom—a kind of poison used to hurt or paralyze enemies

TO LEARN MORE

AT THE LIBRARY

Downs, Kieran. *Praying Mantis vs. Black Widow Spider*. Minneapolis, Minn.: Bellwether Media, 2022.

Loh-Hagan, Virginia. *Deadly Venom*. Ann Arbor, Mich.: Cherry Lake Publishing, 2023.

Mattern, Joanne. *What's So Scary About Spiders?*. South Egremont, Mass.: Red Chair Press LLC, 2022.

ON THE WEB

FACTSURFER

Factsurfer.com gives you a safe, fun way to find more information.

1. Go to www.factsurfer.com

2. Enter "Amazonian giant centipede vs. Brazilian wandering spider" into the search box and click Q.

3. Select your book cover to see a list of related content.

INDEX